A Personal Tour of OLD IRONSIDES

ROBERT YOUNG

⌐ LERNER PUBLICATIONS COMPANY ▪ MINNEAPOLIS

Cover: *The helmsman used this wheel to steer Old Ironsides.*
Title page: *Old Ironsides awaits visitors at Charlestown Naval Yard, Massachusetts.*

Many thanks to Alta Fleming for her help and hospitality; to JO2(SW) Lance Beebe of the United States Navy for making arrangements and contacts; to Mark Berger, Michael Bonanno, and Ann Rand-Grimes of the USS *Constitution* Museum for their generous assistance; to Margherita Desy of the USS *Constitution* Museum for her great patience in answering endless queries; and to Sara and Tyler Young, who help keep the ship afloat.

For the students and staff at Laurel Elementary School, who encourage and celebrate curiosity.

Lerner Publications Company
A division of Lerner Publishing Group
241 First Avenue North
Minneapolis, Minnesota 55401 U.S.A.

Website address: www.lernerbooks.com

LIBRARY OF CONGRESS CATALOGING-IN-PUBLICATION DATA

Young, Robert, 1951–
  Old Ironsides / Robert Young
     p.   cm. – (How it was)
  Includes index.
  Summary: Presents a tour of the American warship in battle during the War of 1812, from the viewpoint of a sailor, passenger, surgeon, and powder monkey.
    ISBN 0-8225-3580-7 (lib. bdg. : alk. paper)
    1. Constitution (Frigate)—Juvenile literature. [1. Constitution (Frigate)]
I. Title. II. Series.
VA65.95′092—dc21
  [B]   99-35500

Manufactured in the United States of America
1 2 3 4 5 6 – JR – 06 05 04 03 02 01

Contents

The USS Constitution *was launched in 1797. The ship rests at the Charlestown Naval Yard after more than two centuries of activity.*

Ship Sails remarkably, and Well and Works Easy.

—James Pity, keeper of the *Constitution*'s journal
on her maiden voyage

Introduction

"Old Ironsides" is the nickname of a famous sailing ship docked at Charlestown Naval Yard in Boston, Massachusetts. The ship—officially known as the USS *Constitution*—was once an important warship in the U.S. Navy. In modern times, Old Ironsides is a popular tourist attraction.

In 1794 the United States was a young nation with a small army and no navy. At that time, privateers (armed, privately owned ships in the service of a country) were attacking U.S. merchant ships as they carried valuable trade goods across the Atlantic Ocean. Congress decided that the merchant ships needed protection and voted to form a navy. They ordered the construction of six **frigates**—high-speed, medium-sized warships.

Joshua Humphreys, of Philadelphia, Pennsylvania, designed the first frigates for the United States. He wanted these ships to be the strongest and fastest warships ever

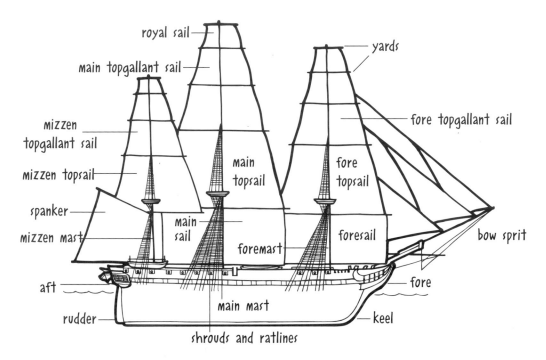

royal sail

main topgallant sail

yards

fore topgallant sail

mizzen
topgallant sail

mizzen topsail

main
topsail

fore
topsail

spanker

mizzen mast

main
sail

foremast

foresail

bow sprit

aft

fore

rudder

main mast

keel

shrouds and ratlines

built. To accomplish this, Humphreys ordered that the best materials be used. Colonel George Claghorne supervised the construction at Edmund Hartt's Boston shipyard.

Workers used oak, the most durable wood available, for most of the ship. The riblike frame of the ship was made of live oak, from trees grown in the southeastern states. White oak formed the ship's backbone, or keel, and was used for the beams and planks that covered the frame to form the **hull** (body) of the ship. The white oak came from the forests of Maine, New Hampshire, Massachusetts, and New Jersey. Rot-resistant yellow pine, from South Carolina and Georgia, was used for the decks. Tall, straight New Hampshire pine trees made the **masts** and **yards,** which supported the sails. The ship was square-rigged, which means that her sails were rectangular. The USS *Constitution* was a forty-four gun boat, carrying forty-four cannons.

The *Constitution* was launched on October 21, 1797. It was the third ship in the U.S. Navy. It was named after the U.S. Constitution, the document that forms the basis of the U.S. government.

The Barbary States—North African regions including Tripoli, Algiers, Morocco, and Tunis—backed many of the corsairs (privateers). In the Mediterranean Sea off Africa's northern coast, the corsairs captured merchant ships, stole the cargoes, and imprisoned sailors. The Barbary States demanded payments, claiming that this would prevent U.S. merchant ships from being attacked. But despite large

The USS *Constitution* cost $302,719 to build. The ship measures 306 feet long and 43 feet, 6 inches at her widest. The assembled height of her main mast is 220 feet tall. She weighs 2,400 tons. The hull of the *Constitution* is 25 inches thick at the waterline. When she was a working warship, she carried fifty to fifty-five guns.

payments and treaties, the corsairs kept attacking American ships. U.S. President Thomas Jefferson eventually refused to pay. The Barbary States then declared war on the United States in 1801.

In response, the U.S. Navy sailed to the Mediterranean Sea. The *Constitution* was the flagship—the ship that carried the commander, then Commodore Edward Preble—for the U.S. Navy squadron during the Barbary War. Under the command of Commodore Edward Preble, the

An eighteenth century painting (above) *shows Old Ironsides engaged in a battle. In the early years of the U.S. Navy, the USS* Constitution *won more battles than any other frigate.*

ship led the charge into the heavily defended harbor at Tripoli. U.S. ships, with their cannons raging, pounded the harbor castle.

In 1805 the Tripolitans surrendered. The Barbary States released U.S. captives, and American merchant ships no longer had to risk corsair attacks. The *Constitution* patrolled the Mediterranean for another year before sailing for home in 1806.

The *Constitution* soon played a role in an ongoing conflict between the United States and Great Britain. After the American Revolution (1775–1783), British forces had remained in U.S. territory along the Great Lakes. Some Americans hoped to conquer Canada and add that land to the United States. Additionally, Great Britain and the United States disagreed on trade restrictions. Great

Britain's navy was blockading (preventing trade with) Europe, so the Royal Navy seized hundreds of U.S. merchant ships carrying goods from Europe. The impressment (forcing into service) of American sailors by the British navy was another issue that divided the two nations.

British naval officers boarded U.S. ships. If they found sailors who had deserted Great Britain's Royal Navy, the British could impress them back into the British navy. But the British navy also impressed British-born American sailors who didn't have papers to prove their U.S. citizenship—and some who did. By the time James Madison became president in 1809, more than two

This drawing details the bombardment of Tripoli's harbor in 1804. The attack helped the United States win the Barbary States War.

thousand U.S. sailors had been impressed into the Royal Navy. By 1812 more Americans were in the British navy than in the U.S. Navy!

A war seemed about to break out. Surely the war would be mainly a naval battle, fought in the Great Lakes and in the Atlantic Ocean. The U.S. forces would be battling the world's most powerful navy, which had six hundred ships. The U.S. Navy had only sixteen ships and supported a number of privateers. But because Great Britain was at war with France, many of the Royal Navy's ships were engaged in battles in faraway European waters.

The British passed laws to change their practices. But before word reached the United States, Congress declared war on Great Britain on June 18, 1812. Under the

James Madison (above), *U.S. president from 1809 to 1817, and Thomas Jefferson* (left), *U.S. president from 1801 to 1809*

command of Captain Isaac Hull, the USS *Constitution* sailed out of the Chesapeake Bay, Maryland, on July 12, 1812. The frigate sailed to join Commodore Rogers' squadron near New York. Off the coast of New Jersey, the *Constitution's* lookouts spotted a fleet of British warships. Greatly outnumbered, Hull had no choice but to sail away. Light winds forced the crew to kedge—a backbreaking task. To kedge, sailors lowered the ship's smaller anchors into boats, which they rowed ahead of the ship. The sailors dropped the anchors and then pulled on the attached cables to pull the ship toward the anchors. Repeating this technique—called walking the ship—again and again, the crew narrowly escaped the British fleet. It took Captain Hull three days of dangerous sailing before the ship was finally safe.

In the U.S. Navy, speakers don't say "the" before a ship's name. They refer to it by just its name. So to follow the official navy rules, call the ship *Constitution*. People who aren't in the navy are used to saying and reading "the" before a vessel's name.

Captain Hull sailed the *Constitution* to Boston Harbor to load supplies. He headed north toward Nova Scotia, part of Great Britain's North American territory, Canada. Along the way, the *Constitution* captured a few small vessels but didn't meet a ship of her own strength.

Come along as we take a close-up view of the USS *Constitution* as the ship patrols the Atlantic waters in search of a single British ship to battle. It's early on the morning of August 19, 1812, in the Atlantic Ocean. The night watch aboard *Constitution* is ending. . . .

The berth deck (above) held sailors' hammocks. The crewmen hung up their hammocks each night and packed them up in the morning.

The Constitution *long shall be,*
The Glory of our Navy....
—The Broadside Ballad

With Ben

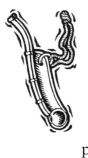

The sound of gunshots woke Ben. He shifted, and his canvas hammock rocked wildly. The night sentries, on the spar deck two decks above, had fired their rifles to signal that it was dawn, time to get up. Ben grimaced as he heard the piercing blast from the boatswain's pipes (whistle). The boatswain, or bos'n, was the sailors' supervisor. With his mates (assistants), the bos'n patrolled the berth deck waking the sailors. As Ben rubbed the sleep from his eyes, the young man looked around. The light from the hanging lanterns was dim, but he could make out the forms of two hundred crewmen swaying in their hammocks. Another two hundred men were on duty in other parts of the ship.

Ben's hammock hung near the bow (the front) of the ship. Ben heard the pigs grunting as they rooted in the straw nearby. He could smell them, too. It wasn't a pleasant smell, though no worse than the sweaty odor of the men in their hammocks. Ben slept near the manger, where live chickens, cows, pigs, and sheep were kept. More live animals were penned near the **galley** (cooking area) on the gun deck. Crates of chickens also filled small boats hanging off the sides of the spar deck. The ship's cooks butchered the animals for food. But Ben and the other seamen never ate the fresh meat, which was served only to the officers on board.

The boatswain's mates walked among the hammocks and shouted at sleeping sailors. The mates hunched forward to keep from hitting their heads on the low ceiling as they rapped slow-moving sailors with thick, knotted pieces of rope called starters. Ben knew the sting of the starter and did not want to feel it again.

Ben rolled out of his hammock and took it down from its hooks. He pulled on his shirt and began to wind his canvas hammock into a tight roll. Most of the other men were

When the men weren't sleeping, it was important to keep the berth deck clear. In a battle, the ship's surgeon used this area to treat wounded seamen. The sick bay, located in the most forward area of the berth deck, didn't have enough space. Sailors aboard the *Constitution* and other warships of the time stored their hammocks on the spar deck.

Another reason to stow the hammocks on the topmost deck was to protect the sailors on board. The hammocks piled along the **bulwark** made it harder for enemy sharpshooters (snipers) to aim at the crew on the spar deck. The hammocks also absorbed flying splinters when cannonballs hit a wooden ship.

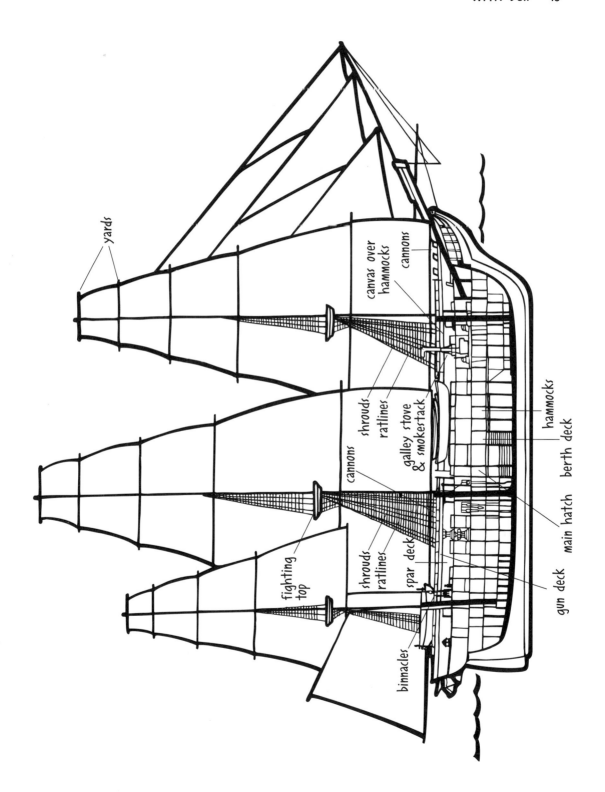

yards

canvas over hammocks

cannons

shrouds ratlines

galley stove & smokestack

cannons

fighting top

shrouds ratlines

spar deck

binnacles

hammocks

berth deck

main hatch

gun deck

The USS *Constitution* has four decks. The top deck, called the spar deck, is open to the weather. The gun deck with its gun ports and cannons stretches right below the spar deck. Below is the berth deck, where most of the crew slept and ate their meals. The lowest deck is the orlop deck, which the crew used to store supplies. Below the orlop deck is another storage area known as the hold, the lowest part of the ship.

dressing or rolling their hammocks. A few slept on, but not for long. The boatswain shoved the sleeping sailors out of their hammocks, and the men thumped onto the hard wooden deck. The sailors had only twelve minutes to dress, stow their hammocks, and report for duty.

Ben grabbed his rolled hammock and pushed through the crowd to the companionway, the steps that led from one deck to the next. He ran up the steps to the gun deck and glanced at the deck's shiny black cannons. Ben greeted the two men working the levers of the **bilge**-pump, which brought up seawater that had leaked into the bottom of the hold. The dirty bilgewater flowed across the deck and out the small holes drilled in the sides of the ship. By regular pumping, the amount of water in the bilge could be kept down to about two inches.

Ben ran up the next set of steep steps to the spar deck. He took a deep breath. The damp, salty air was a relief after the stench of the berth deck. Ben carried his rolled hammock to the netting that lined the larboard (left) bulwark. Here the side of the ship rose above the spar deck like a short wall, which formed the bulwark. He stowed his hammock in the netting. Then he helped pull a canvas cover over the top of the netting. Ben had a few minutes before he had to report for duty. He ran along the deck to the bow, where he ducked through a square opening along the wall. He reached the wooden seat with a hole that opened to the ocean below. It was one of the heads, or bathrooms, on the ship. After using the head, Ben was ready to begin his daily duties.

Ben started on the watch below. Instead of working to sail the ship, the members of the watch below kept the ship clean and in good working order. They wiped unpainted wood to keep it free of salt. They rubbed brass and copper fittings with a mixture of ashes and grease. The blend kept the metal shiny and removed the greenish tinge caused by corrosion.

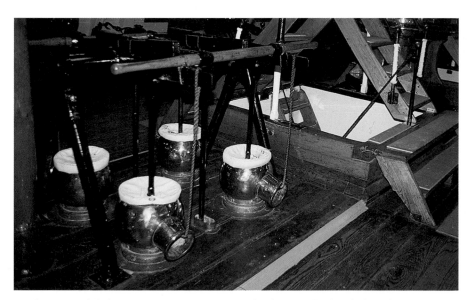

Sailors used bilge-pumps (above) *on the lower deck of the ship to pump seawater out of the hold.*

An officer assigned Ben and other sailors to the ship's stern, or back part, to wipe the wood with rags. They passed other sailors tossing buckets of water on the deck. Soon these men were on their hands and knees, scrubbing the deck with large, flat holystones.

Bored as he performed his job on the watch below, Ben watched the helmsman, who had an interesting and important task. He maneuvered the ship with the **helm,** a large wooden steering wheel. On the deck in front of the wheel were two cases, called **binnacles,** displaying the ship's compasses. The captain used a compass to set the sailing **course.** The helmsman followed the captain's plan, using compasses to help him stay on course. Ben wished he were standing behind the wheel of the ship instead of collecting salt in his rag.

In a few hours, the ship's bell rang eight times and the boatswain blasted his pipes. It was time for breakfast. Ben quickly wrung out his rag, then he ran down the steps of the hatchway to the gun deck and down to the berth deck. Sailors gathered around painted pieces of canvas arranged on the floor. Ben found his eight-man mess (the group he always ate with) in its usual spot. The cook of Ben's mess had set pans, plates, utensils, and cups on the canvas. Ben and his messmates sat on the deck around the canvas. They talked while they waited for the cook to bring their food. Soon the cook came with their tea and hardtack (biscuits).

Sailors sanded the deck to keep it clean. They used heavy, flat pieces of sandstone, called holystones because each stone was about the size of a Bible. And to use them, the men had to be on their knees as if they were praying.

The helmsman steered the ship by turning the wheel. Heavy ropes attached to the drum of the wheel ran beneath the decks to a huge wooden beam called the tiller. The tiller connected to the rudder, a large flat piece of wood that plunged into the water at the back of the ship. By maneuvering the wheel, the helmsman could swing the rudder to turn the ship.

Ben split a biscuit in half and banged it against the deck. Small gray bugs—weevil grubs—fell out. The young sailor ate his meal as fast as he could, trying not to taste whatever bugs still remained in the biscuit.

The shrill sound of the boatswain's whistle soon filled the air, signaling that breakfast was over. The crowd of seamen moved up the steps to the upper decks. They left the mess cooks the chore of cleaning up after the meal.

Ben returned to the spar deck, where he was assigned to work aloft (high above the deck). Ben loved this duty. Short ropes, called ratlines, linked two sturdy shrouds (lines) supporting the mast. Ben was the first up the ratlines. He climbed on the windward side of the shrouds. The light sea breeze pushed him into the **rigging,** which

The rigging is the system of ropes, called lines, that sailors use to help sail a ship. There are two types of rigging—standing rigging and running rigging. Standing rigging is fixed, or unchanging. The shrouds are part of the standing rigging.

Running rigging is not fixed. It includes the lines sailors use to change the sails. Beyond the bow is the bowsprit, a large pole that extends out over the water. Rigging connects it to the front mast, or foremast, to keep it in place. Rigging from the center main (the main mast) links to the foremast. Rigging also connects the mizzenmast (rear mast) to the main mast.

made climbing easier and safer. Partway up the mast, Ben reached the fighting top, a platform where the onboard marines would act as sharpshooters during a battle.

Like most of the *Constitution*'s crew, Ben pulled himself up from the outside edges of the fighting top. Inexperienced sailors and crewmen afraid of falling used the lubber's hole, an opening on the inside of the fighting top near the mast.

Up, up, and up. Ben climbed the next ratline, higher into the rigging. Far above the deck, he became more careful with each step. He had seen men fall from this height to the deck below. A few had died from the fall. The others were very badly injured.

Ben was only one of many men working aloft. Some sailors carried a needle and thread to sew tears in the sails. Others worked at loosing (letting out) and furling (taking in) the sails closest to the deck of the ship. Ben and others skilled at climbing aloft were assigned to the **topsail** and rigging. Ben liked the danger and excitement of being so high above the water.

As the *Constitution* rolled and pitched, Ben sat on the uppermost yard, a horizontal wooden pole that supports a sail. He watched the men at work below him, and then he gazed over the ocean. It sparkled in the morning sun.

It was a peaceful day. But Ben knew that enemy ships had been spotted in the area. The *Constitution* would be in a battle soon.

The USS *Constitution* is equipped with thirty-six sails. The area of those sails would cover about one acre of land. Most of the time, about fourteen sails were enough to keep the ship moving. During battle, the vessel required only six sails.

Carronades—short, fat cannons—line both sides of the Constitution's spar deck. The carronades could fire 42-pound cannonballs.

*It is not difficult for refined
women to dwell upon the deep....*

—Moses Smith,
seaman aboard the USS *Constitution*

With Mary

Safe in her small home near Boston Harbor, Mary read the article on the newspaper's front page with concern. The article was about the USS *Constitution*, a ship on which she had once sailed. Mary read that the *Constitution* had recently sailed into the Atlantic Ocean to protect the coast from British warships.

A few years back, the ship had carried civilian passengers, including Mary and her husband, Thomas. At that time, Thomas, who worked for the U. S. government, and Mary were staying in the Netherlands. Thomas attended meetings with other government officials while he was there. Near the end of their stay, the *Constitution* docked, carrying money the United States owed to the Dutch government. Thomas and Mary received permission to sail aboard the *Constitution* on her return voyage to the United States.

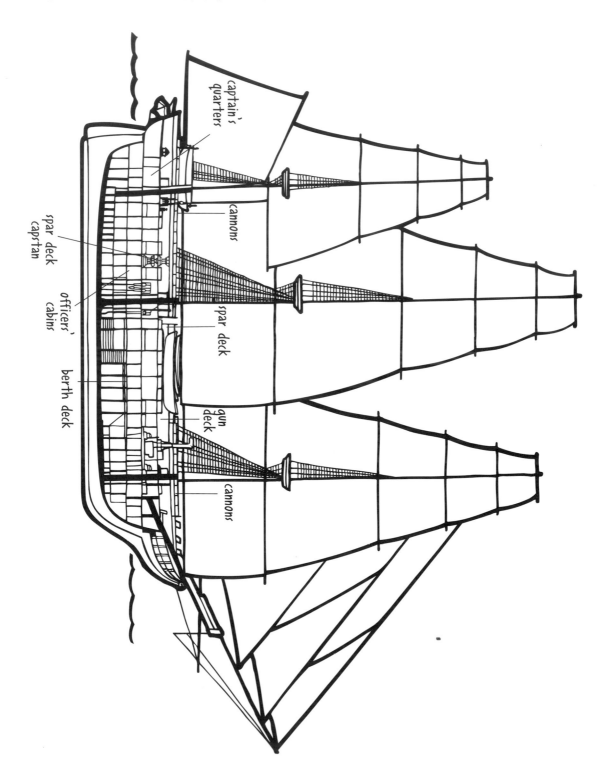

captain's
quarters

cannons

spar deck
capstan

officers'
cabins

berth deck

spar deck

gun
deck

cannons

On a clear sunny day, Mary and Thomas walked from the dock up a wooden **gangplank** to the USS *Constitution*. Mary grabbed Thomas's arm as they walked along the narrow boards high above the water. Feeling steadier, she looked up at the masts that rose like tall trees above the deck.

At the top of the gangplank, a sailor took hold of her other arm and assisted her down onto the spar deck. A lieutenant ordered one of the sailors to show Mary and Thomas to their quarters. Before the sailor took them below, he walked with them along the spar deck. The deck buzzed with activity. Sailors tugged on lines, scrubbed the deck, and cleaned the stubby cannons that lined the ship. Mary winced at the strong odor of tar and looked for the source of the smell. She soon spotted a small group of sailors at work painting dark brown tar on the standing rigging.

Clang-clang! Clang-clang! Near the main mast rising from the deck, a sailor rang a bronze bell hanging from a wooden frame. Mary liked the rich sound of the bell. She knew the bell was not on board for its musical sound but to tell the crew the time. Mary wondered how they knew when to ring the bell. The sailor explained that a sentry stood guard near the captain's quarters. The sentry watched the sand in a sandglass. When the sand ran out after half an hour, the sentry turned the glass over. Then the sentry reported to the spar deck, where an officer ordered the bell to be rung. The sentry went back to his post, where he measured the next half hour. The sailor said to Mary that, on a ship, the day began at noon instead of at midnight.

The sailor led Mary and Thomas forward along the spar deck. They passed the capstan, a large winch (a crank with a handle for pulling up rope). The crew was able to work the rigging by pushing bars into the sides of the capstan, then turning it.

Not far from the capstan, Mary saw the deck's main hatch, a large opening leading to the ship's other decks. Sailors were lowering supplies through the main hatch. The sailors had looped ropes over the yards (poles supporting sails) above. They held one end of the rope and attached the other to a sack of flour. They eased the sack down through the main hatch. Next they lowered a barrel packed with gunpowder and then heavy oak barrels of nails, dried peas, and fresh, drinkable water. Mary stopped to watch the heavy oak barrels disappear. Her guide told her that sailors would lower the supplies through hatches in the gun deck and the berth deck to the orlop deck. He said that barrels of oatmeal, cheese, and fresh water would be lowered into the hold.

The sailor led Mary and Thomas to their cabins two decks below, in the **aft** (back) section of the berth deck. Mary was relieved when she saw that her cabin was right

> Tar, the pitch or resin from trees, was essential to maintaining wooden ships like the *Constitution*. Sailors painted the molasses-like liquid onto the standing rigging. The lines were made of hemp, a natural fiber that was not water-resistant. Tarring the lines protected them from the seawater, which over time could cause the lines to rot and snap. Sailors spent so much time using tar that the word became a nickname for sailors.

Time is organized differently on a ship than on land. Each twenty-four hour day is divided into six equal parts of four hours. Each four-hour period is called a watch, and jobs on board the ship are organized around the watches.

The midnight watch runs from midnight to 4 A.M. After the first half hour, a sailor rings the ship's bell one time. After the next half hour, the bell is rung twice. This continues each half hour until eight bells have been rung. That is the end of the day's first four-hour watch. The process begins again for the next watch, working up to eight bells, and continues throughout the day in the same way.

next to her husband's cabin. The cabins were so small that Mary wondered how the officers could live in them for the many months they were at sea. She was surprised to find room for more than the short, narrow bed built against the wall. A sailor had delivered her small clothes trunk, which sat on the wooden floor.

Mary unlatched her trunk. She pulled out a small rug, unrolled it, and placed it on the floor. She liked adding touches of home, no matter where she was. She was glad to be going back to Boston—a few weeks' journey—and felt thankful that the ship's officers had made space for them in the cabins. She knew that she would spend a great deal of time in this room.

But Mary liked to stay on the spar deck as much as she could. There she could smell the salt air and look out over the glistening ocean. She watched the sailors climb high into the rigging above the deck. She listened to the sails snap in the wind. Best of all, she loved the gentle rocking motion of the ship as it rose and fell among the waves.

Like other government officials sailing on the *Constitution*, Thomas dined with Captain Hull. Mary joined them in the great cabin, which was part of the captain's quarters in the aft section of the gun deck. The room spanned the width of the ship. The polished timber floor shone. In the center of the cabin, elegant chairs surrounded a long wooden table. Against the back wall, a beautiful cabinet held dishware and utensils.

Each evening, Mary and Thomas sat at the long table with the captain's other guests. Beyond the small round windows at the ends of the cabin, the sky darkened as evening approached. Members of the crew entered from the front of the room. They carried platters of food, which had been prepared in the small area just outside the great cabin. Mary had been surprised at the good food, and she had enjoyed the captain's interesting conversation. Mary had wished those evenings would never end.

On one occasion, Captain Hull showed Mary and Thomas his private quarters. Captain Hull led them

he gun deck was full of
l prepared for wounded men.

The officers' quarters included small cabins to sleep in and a place to socialize (above).

through a small door next to the cabinet at the back of the great cabin. The door's shiny brass handle was so smooth that it felt slippery.

Captain Hull showed them his day cabin, where he spent much of his time. It was cozy and smaller than the great cabin. The captain invited them to sit on his couch. The cushioned bench ran along the wall that separated the day cabin from the great cabin.

The back of the day cabin was the hull of the ship. Three square windows looked out over the ocean. In the center of the cabin, Mary saw a map spread open across a table. The captain told Mary that he relied on the map to track the ship's location and to plot its course. He wrote

about each day's events in the ship's journal at t
wooden desk against a side wall.

Before Mary and Thomas returned to their quarte
Captain Hull opened a door on the side of the day cal
and showed them his tiny stateroom. His bed was bu
into one wall, and he kept his clothes in drawers bu
into a corner. On the opposite side of the stateroom, a
opening led to the small night cabin with its bench an
many windows. Captain Hull remarked that an identic
stateroom was on the other side of the great cabin. Th
commodore, the captain's commanding officer, used th

The captain's quarters (above, through the windows) *are tucked in the*
ship's hull. The quarters include a great cabin, day cabin, and
stateroom.

As the Constitution *prepared for battle,*
activity. Crewmen tended to cannons an

Her deck...
Where knelt the vanquished foe,
When winds were hurrying o'er the flood
And waves were white below....
—Oliver Wendell Holmes, "Old Ironsides"

With Surgeon Martin

Surgeon James Martin leaned against a cannon and looked aft along the gun deck. It was a busy place in the morning. Some sailors were blackening the cannons. Other crewmen sat between the cannons, doing other daily chores.

The sail maker sat on the deck and sewed a canvas sail. Others worked on a smaller piece of canvas that would cover the floor of the cockpit (medical room) floor when Surgeon Martin tended to men wounded during battle. The cordwainer (leather worker) stitched a leather bucket used to carry gunpowder to the cannons during battle. The cooper whistled as he mended a barrel.

With a hatchetlike tool, the ship's carpenter shaped wooden plugs. During a battle, enemy cannons might blast a hole in the body of the *Constitution*. If that happened, sailors would fill the hole with a wooden plug.

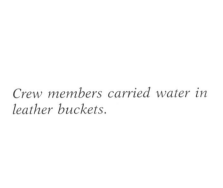

Crew members carried water in leather buckets.

Surgeon Martin nodded hello to the carpenter. Their jobs were really quite similar. As the ship's surgeon, James Martin was responsible for the physical well-being of the crew. The carpenter was in charge of the physical well-being of the ship. Keeping the USS *Constitution* afloat was his responsibility. He fixed leaks, repaired battle damage, and replaced rotted wood.

Surgeon Martin noticed that, as usual, a sailor sat in the barber's chair near the forward hatch, or companionway. The barber and his assistant shaved each sailor twice a week and the officers every day. Beyond the barber's chair was the galley. James could see cooks at the big, black stove in the middle of the deck. One cook prepared a roast over the stove's open fire for the officers' midday meal. A cook sampled salt beef stew from the sunken pots

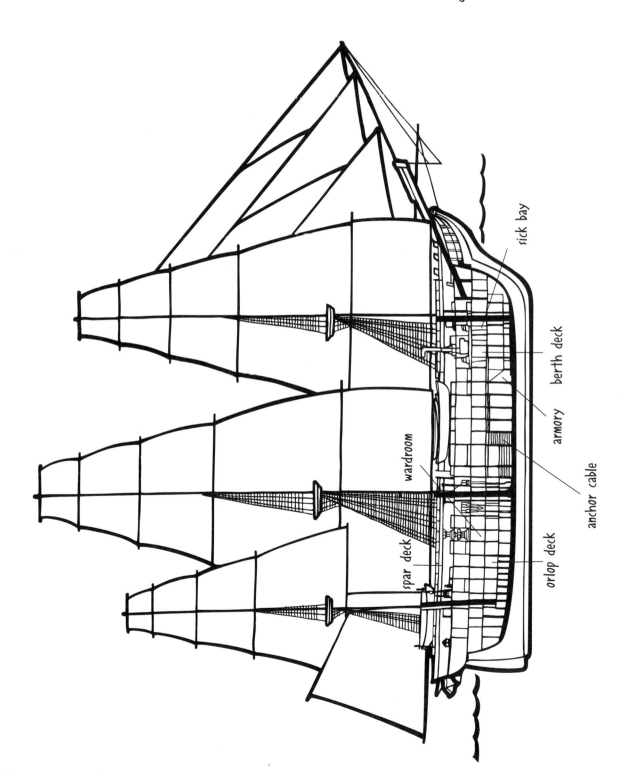

sick bay

berth deck

armory

anchor cable

orlop deck

wardroom

spar deck

Why did the barber have to shave all the men on board the *Constitution*? Why didn't the men shave themselves? Like many ships' captains, the captain of the *Constitution* did not allow crew members to have razors. He was afraid the men would use the razors as weapons against each other.

on the other side of the stove. The stew would be the midday meal for the sailors.

As Surgeon Martin watched the activity on the deck, the shrill piping of the boatswain filled the air. After the whistle came the shouting of boatswain's mates calling the crew to watch a punishment on the spar deck.

Surgeon Martin hurried up to the top deck, where he joined a crowd of men. The officer in charge gave the order to rig the grates (flat surfaces of interlaced strips of wood) that covered the hatches. A pair of sailors lifted two grates from the hatches. They lay one flat on the deck. They placed the other one against the bulwark in an upright position.

The master-at-arms (the ship's police officer) led two young men to the grates and ordered the sailors to take off the men's shirts. Then the master-at-arms tied the men to the upright grate. He announced the charges against the men—neglect of duty. They had been sleeping when they should have been working.

A boatswain's mate pulled the cat-o'-nine-tails whip from a red cloth bag. The whip's long handle split into nine strips of leather, like nine cats' tails. On command, the mate began to flog (whip) the men. Crack! Whack!

A modern-day life buoy hangs on the spar deck, where the master-at-arms flogged disobedient sailors.

Crack! Twelve lashes of the whip brought bloody streaks to the men's bare backs.

Surgeon Martin was relieved when the flogging ended. He knew that discipline on board a ship was necessary. It was important to punish men who didn't follow the rules. Still, he didn't enjoy watching people being beaten. And he didn't look forward to cleaning and bandaging the wounds, which often became infected.

The phrase "letting the cat out of the bag" comes from the days when sailors were flogged with a cat-o'-nine-tails, which was stored in a bag. The crew knew someone was going to be punished when they saw the "cat" come out of the bag. The phrase means "to make a secret known."

At last the bell sounded for the midday meal. After two long whistles from the boatswain's pipes, the watch below stopped work. The crew moved to its mess areas. Surgeon Martin ate with other officers in the wardroom aft of the berth deck. The officers' cabins lined the sides of the wardroom.

Surgeon Martin sat on one of the benches along the wooden table. As sailors served the officers' meal, the surgeon looked at the sailors eating on the berth deck. The men's voices were louder than usual today, and Martin sensed excitement in the air. Everyone seemed to feel that a battle was near. The officers spoke quietly. They knew that their ship, their crew, and they themselves would be tested soon.

After the meal, Surgeon Martin strolled along the berth deck. He walked past the manger to the forward part of the ship until he reached the sick bay. Wooden grates separated the small, triangular sick bay from the rest of the deck. In spite of the lanterns, the area was still dim. Several wood-framed bunks hung from ropes attached to the overhead (ceiling) and gently rocked as the ship moved. In the bunks, one man snored. Another hacked and coughed. In a corner bunk, a man moaned as he turned over. One of the surgeon's mates tended to the sick men.

Surgeon Martin stepped into the room to begin his rounds. He stopped at the bunks to examine each patient.

Ill and wounded crewmen received aid in the sick bay.

The midday meal was the one hot meal served to the men aboard the *Constitution*. Usually, the meal was a meat-and-vegetable stew ordered by the captain. To prevent food from spoiling on the long sea voyages, the cooks dried vegetables and bought meat pickled in brine, a heavily salted water. The salted meat would be soaked in fresh water for hours before being served. But even so, these foods tasted best when cooked together in a stew. Grog tubs like this one stored water and food on the orlop deck.

He took each man's pulse and looked at his tongue. He made notes in a small book and gave orders to the mate. One man needed his bandages changed. Another needed a cool wet rag to help lower his fever.

Surgeon Martin came to a man who needed to be bled. The surgeon pulled up a stool, poked the man's arm with a sharp, needlelike instrument, and watched the blood drain into a basin. After about a pint of blood had flowed from the man, Surgeon Martin pressed on the wound to stop the blood flow. Then he bandaged it. Surgeon Martin would take another pint from the man tomorrow. He hoped that it would help the sailor recover.

Doctors in the early 1800s believed that bleeding, or taking blood from, sick patients could help cure them. Bleeding was believed to relieve tension on arteries and to allow poisons to drain out of the body.

When he left the sick bay, James took a lantern from the rafters. The light flickered as he descended the steep steps to the orlop deck. This deck was used mainly for storing food and other supplies. It also

The sick bay (above) *was an area for ill or wounded crewmen to receive aid.*

housed the cockpit, where the surgeon and his crew worked on injured sailors.

As Surgeon Martin made his way to the front of the ship, he climbed up and down several short stairways. He passed large, open areas storing coiled anchor cable.

Small storage rooms lined the deck. Barrels of molasses and vinegar filled some rooms. Others were packed with large bags bulging with rice, sugar, and flour, with chests of pistols and cutlasses (swords), and with cannonballs. Folded canvas sails filled another area. Nearby, the yeoman, who was in charge of the ship's supplies, maintained a small, lantern-lit magazine (storage room). The sailors visited the magazine when they needed an item from the ship's store of supplies.

Sailors took special precautions with the oil lamps lighting the magazine. They placed the lamps in copper boxes with glass windows outside the magazine. They did this so that sparks from a flame would not ignite the gunpowder and cause an explosion.

Near the middle of the ship, Surgeon Martin came upon a large area where the floor opened to the hold below. Here, one sailor held a lantern while two more knelt on the deck and lowered a weighted line into the lowest part of the ship. These men were "sounding the hold." Each day, they checked how much water had leaked into the ship. Some leakage was expected, but sometimes there was more water than usual. The sailors reported their findings to the ship's carpenter, who was in charge of repairing any holes or cracks in the body of the ship.

Rats scurried past Surgeon Martin as he continued

along the orlop deck. Soon he reached the cockpit, a 16-foot-long room tucked away where it would be safe from enemy fire. The cabins along the sides of the cockpit were the living quarters for the surgeon's mates. He hung his lantern on a peg and the room lit up.

The cockpit was neatly arranged. The painted red floor had been swept carefully. A folded sheet of canvas lay in the corner for use in the amputation area, in the center of the room. Surgeon Martin was often called upon to re-move a wounded sailor's arm or leg when the limb was injured beyond repair. A small table held Surgeon Martin's tools. There lay knives, saws, and a tourniquet—a device for wrapping around an arm or leg to stop bleeding. Buckets of sand lined one wall. Surgeon Martin placed amputated body parts into the buckets. Later, a surgeon's mate would throw the limbs overboard.

As Dr. Martin finished inspecting the cockpit, one of his mates rushed in. He excitedly reported that a sailor on the watch aloft had spotted a ship on the horizon. It might be a British **man-of-war!** If it was, a battle would soon follow.

Surgeon Martin moved quickly. He sprinkled sand from one of the buckets across the floor. The sand would keep the floor from becoming slippery with blood. This small room would become important once the battle began.

The *Constitution* contained 700 feet of rope known as anchor cable, measuring 22 inches around. When the ship was not at anchor, crewmen untied the cable from the capstan and stored the cable on the orlop deck.

This view from the deck of Old Ironsides looks out onto the Atlantic Ocean.

And now begun the bloody fray,
The balls flew thick and hot sir,
In half-an-hour the job was done.
The Guerrière *went to pot sir!*
                                —*The Broadside Ballad*

With Samuel

Samuel stretched to see past the men kneeling on the berth deck in front of him. Looking between the heads of the men, Samuel could see the black circle drawn on deck with charcoal from the ship's stove. Inside the circle, weevil grubs moved about. The men cheered loudly as the insects skittered toward the charcoal outline.

Samuel had heard about these games, but he had never seen them until he came to work aboard the ship. The sailors picked the insects from their food, placed the bugs in the center of the charcoal circle, and let them go. They watched and cheered as the grubs wandered. The first weevil to leave the charcoal circle was the winner.

Some of the men bet on which weevil would win. But not Samuel, who never bet. As one of the ship's boys, he only earned about half as much money as the sailors did.

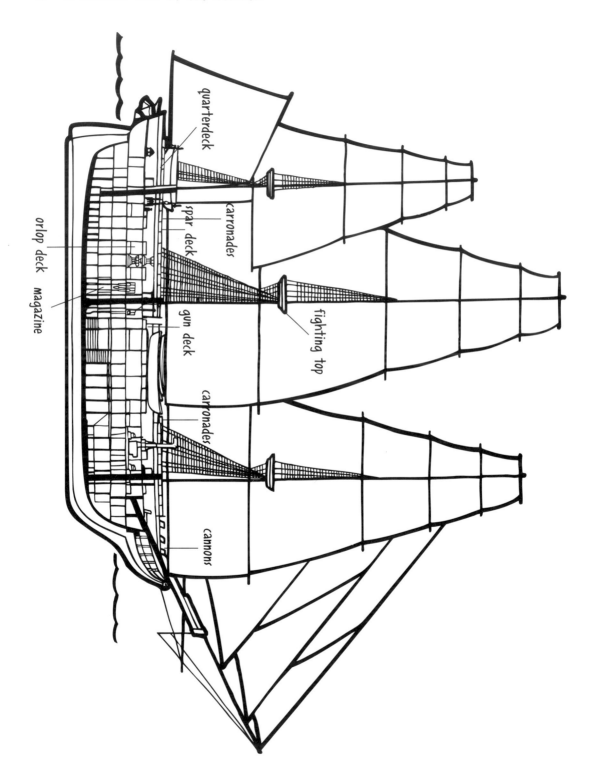

quarterdeck

spar deck

carronades

orlop deck

magazine

gun deck

fighting top

carronades

cannons

And he was saving every penny of his pay for his parents back in Boston.

Besides Samuel, several boys between the ages of ten and eighteen served on board the *Constitution*. Officers on board assigned duties to the boys. They worked as sentries to keep the ship's time, and they carried messages. During a battle, the boys performed the dangerous job of powder monkey. They carried gunpowder from the magazine on the orlop deck to the cannons on the top two decks. Samuel hadn't experienced a battle yet. But another boy had told him that a single spark was all it took to ignite and explode the gunpowder the boys carried. Samuel had also been told that sharpshooters knew the importance of powder monkeys and often targeted the boys.

As one of the grub weevils made it out of the circle, Samuel cheered along with the other sailors.

The name "powder monkey" came about because the young crew members had to be agile, like monkeys, to run very fast from the gun deck to the magazine, where the powder was stored. It was important to quickly get the gunpowder to the men who fired the cannons. The gunpowder was stored far from the gun deck to make sure that sparks didn't ignite the explosive substance.

Samuel enjoyed this break from work. Each morning before an officer assigned him a job, Samuel did his school lessons. Sometimes his task was to keep time with the sandglass, but mostly he was assigned to scrub the gun deck with a holystone. Scrubbing the deck was safe but boring. Samuel often wished for the excitement of battle.

Samuel grinned when he realized that he might get his wish. Sailors ran down the hatchway and onto the berth deck, shouting that a large ship had been sighted. Up on the spar deck, men worked to identify the ship. Was it a friend or an enemy? Samuel shuddered with excitement and fear as he followed the pack of men. They raced to the top deck, pushed to the rail, and stared at the horizon. Samuel easily spotted the approaching ship a few miles away, its white sails billowing. Near the crowded rail, the first officer looked through a spyglass and spoke quietly to the captain. Soon an officer shouted for all hands (sailors) on deck. In the rigging above, topmen began to loose, or unroll, the sails that were tied to the yards. Word passed among the crew that *Constitution* was sailing toward the **HMS** *Guerrière*, a British frigate. She was a fierce fighting ship and a proud part of the most powerful navy in the world. Samuel could see that the British ship had taken in sail and turned, awaiting the *Constitution*. A battle was certain!

Drumbeats cut through the air. The drummers tapped the "beat to quarters" call, warning the crew to prepare the ship for battle. The bo'sun's mates raced up and down the spar deck shouting orders. Everyone on board the *Constitution* had a job. Samuel was assigned to be the powder monkey for two carronades on the quarterdeck, the aft section of the spar deck.

As Samuel ran to his carronades, he watched the sailors quickly and quietly perform their duties. He was glad that Captain Hull had arranged for so many hours of practice. Crewmen began clearing the decks to allow more space to maneuver during battle. They dragged the mess

The spar deck saw much of the ship's wartime activity. When sailors spotted enemy ships from high up in the lines, their crewmates rushed to fire cannons.

chests and other objects into the hold. Other men pulled up buckets of seawater. They threw some of the water onto the decks to help prevent fires and filled tubs with water to pour on any fires that might flare up. Then sailors spread sand and ashes across the decks. This would help prevent the crew from slipping.

At Samuel's carronades, a gun captain told Samuel to bring gunpowder from the magazine as quickly as possible. Samuel grabbed two leather buckets and ran along the deck. Before going down the companionway to the lower decks, he saw marines climbing the rigging to the fighting top. From there, the sharpshooters would fire their rifles down at the deck of the enemy ship. The trouble was that the *Guerrière's* sharpshooters would be firing down at the *Constitution*. This thought made Samuel run a little faster through the lower decks of the ship.

On the gun deck, the wheels of the heavy cannons rumbled as crews moved them into position. He passed sailors lugging wooden chests up from below. Some chests held muskets. Others held the cutlasses the sailors would wield if they were called to board the *Guerrière*.

Down on the berth deck, everything had been cleared away. Samuel recalled that the surgeon would use this area, as well as the cockpit, to treat sailors wounded during battle. Finally, Samuel reached the magazine. Wet woolen blankets hung in the doorway to the powder room. The wet blankets were between the explosive powder and sparks flying from lanterns or cannon fire.

Loosing (untying) the sails allowed a ship to move faster. (The force of wind pushing at the sails makes a sailing vessel move.) For extra speed, the captain ordered the watch above to loose the sails. Sailors stood on ropes below the yards to untie the lines that had bound the sails. When the captain wanted to slow the ship, he ordered sails furled. Sailors neatly gathered the canvas sails and then tightly tied them to the yard.

Samuel parted the blankets and squinted into the tiny space. He could make out the shapes of two men quickly filling cartridges (sacks of gunpowder) for the powder monkeys at the door. One of the men passed Samuel cartridges. The boy put them into leather buckets and scampered to the spar deck. At the carronades, the gun crews unloaded boxes that carried the shot for the guns. Samuel saw every kind of shot he could imagine. He wondered what would be used on this day.

Samuel watched one of the gun crews at work. The five men worked as a team to fire a carronade. One man loaded the cannon by pushing a cartridge down the barrel. From the cannon's other side, another man used a ramrod to shove the cartridge into place at the bottom of the barrel. He then placed a round shot into the barrel,

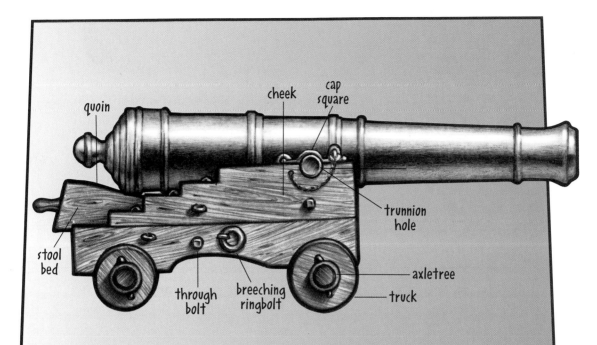

The crew of the *Constitution* used cannonballs, known as round shot, to fire from cannons and carronades. These heavy round balls were made of iron. But cannonballs were not the only shot fired by cannons and carronades. Chain shot, heavy balls joined by a chain, was used to destroy rigging of enemy ships. Grapeshot, a canvas bag filled with small iron balls, was fired at enemy sailors. Canister shot was a metal cylinder containing small pieces of glass and metal. This type of shot could wound enemy sailors or land on the deck of the enemy ship, which would make it more dangerous for the barefoot sailors to move around.

The cannons of Old Ironsides fired round shots (left) *and canister shots* (right).

quickly rammed it in, and jammed in a piece of rope to keep the shot from falling out.

At the back of the carronade, a sailor poked a stiff wire through the fuse hole and punctured the powder cartridge. To make a fuse, he placed a quill (feather) filled with gunpowder into the hole. The fuse would carry the flame to the cartridge. The gunpowder would explode, forcing the shot out of the barrel. A sailor used a wedge-shaped block of wood, called a quoin, to raise the back end of the barrel. The crew used ropes to help drag the gun into firing position. It was ready to fire.

Samuel knew what to expect. The crew had practiced so many times. The gun captain would light the fuse, the men would cover their ears and jump out of the way, and BOOM! The carronade would blast its shot at the enemy ship. The explosion would jerk the gun backward against the ropes. Then the crew would leap forward and roll the gun back into position. Even a tiny ember could cause an explosion when the sailors were reloading the cannon. So one of the gun crew would ram a wet swab down the inside of the barrel to dampen any sparks.

The carronade and all the other cannons on the two top decks of the *Constitution* sat ready to be fired. Although the ship's long guns could reach a target about 1,300 yards away and the carronades shot about 400 yards, Captain Hull held fire until the *Guerrière* was closer. The nearer the *Constitution* was to the enemy ship, the more damage the shots would do.

The sailors grew quiet. Samuel listened to the timbers creaking, the canvas flapping, and the waves slapping against the hull.

The *Guerrière* fired first. Shots whizzed through the *Constitution*'s rigging. A few jarred the hull. Samuel held his breath. The ship sailed closer to *Guerrière*. Finally, Captain Hull gave the order to fire. The thunderous explosion blasted Samuel's eardrums and nearly knocked him off his feet. The gun captain shouted for more powder. Samuel ran down the steps, through thick clouds of smoke, and past the excited men. Bullets from the *Guerrière*'s sharpshooters whizzed around him. Splinters filled the air. The *Constitution*'s cannons boomed. The vessels were almost touching. Samuel knew sea battles did not last long. He hoped he would be on the winning side.

This period lithograph by Nathaniel Currier depicts Old Ironsides (above right) *successfully battling the HMS* Guerrière.

During the nineteenth century, the USS Constitution *played many roles in the U.S. Navy. This image shows the ship under repair in 1858.*

Now safe in Boston port we're moored ...
And every true American
With loud huzzahs shall greet us.
—The Broadside Ballad

Afterword

The battle between the USS *Constitution* and the HMS *Guerrière* didn't last long. Less than an hour after the *Constitution* began firing, the captain of the *Guerrière* surrendered. His ship was destroyed. The *Constitution* had wrecked the ship's sails and rigging. Holes riddled the body of the vessel, and its masts were toppled. The crew suffered 101 casualties out of its 302 men. By comparison, the *Constitution* had only 7 casualties and 7 wounded from its crew of 456.

The HMS *Guerrière* was damaged beyond repair. The Americans transferred the British survivors onto the *Constitution*, then set the *Guerrière's* powder magazine on fire, blowing up the ship. She quickly sank into the North Atlantic.

The defeat of the *Guerrière* shocked the British. Their navy was the most powerful in the world. The *Constitution's*

During this battle, the USS *Constitution* got her nickname "Old Ironsides." As the cannonballs from the *Guerrière* bounced off the thick wooden hull of the *Constitution*, one of the ship's sailors shouted, "Huzzah! Her sides are made of iron!" Although cannonballs did cause some damage to the *Constitution*, the ship soon became known as Old Ironsides.

victory lifted the spirits of Americans, who had been suffering discouraging losses to the British on land. This victory at sea also helped create support among Americans for expanding the navy. Within a year, Congress authorized four ships of the line with seventy-four guns each. These were the U.S. Navy's most powerful vessels. The navy also ordered six forty-four-gun frigates and several smaller vessels.

Despite the victory of Old Ironsides against the *Guerrière*, the War of 1812 continued. Battles were waged on land and at sea. In the west, Indians joined British troops to defeat the Americans. Losses continued for the United States until the Americans, under the command of William Henry Harrison, defeated the British at the Battle of Thames, near Lake Erie in Canada.

Other British forces attacked Washington, D.C., where they set fire to government buildings, including the White House. The British continued on to Baltimore, where they attacked Fort McHenry at dawn on September 13, 1814. The attack continued throughout the day and into the night. As Americans successfully defended the fort, the Washington lawyer Francis Scott Key watched and wrote the words to "The Star-Spangled Banner," which later became the national anthem.

By the time General Andrew Jackson defeated the British forces at the Battle of New Orleans, the war was officially over. American and British representatives signed a peace treaty in Ghent, Belgium, on December 14, 1814. Word of the agreement took several weeks to reach the troops fighting in America, and many died tragically after the treaty was signed. The terms of peace were very simple. The fighting was to stop. No territory would change hands.

Old Ironsides was victorious in each of her thirty-three engagements over the fifty-six years she served as a warship. After her days as a war ship, the *Constitution* had many other important jobs. Between 1844 and 1846, she sailed around the world with crews that developed trade partners, established coaling stations for U.S. steamships,

Old Ironsides was docked off the coast of Massachusetts in 1897.

collected seeds and plants for scientific study, and gathered information about other nations.

From 1853 to 1855, the *Constitution* became part of the African Squadron. This group of U.S. warships enforced the law that made the slave trade illegal for American ships. Operating off the western coast of Africa, the crew of Old Ironsides inspected American merchant ships to make sure that they were not carrying slaves.

During the middle of the 1800s, the navy replaced most of its sailing vessels with steamships. In 1860 Old Ironsides began to serve as a classroom, dorm, and training ship for students at the U.S. Naval Academy in Annapolis, Maryland.

The *Constitution* later served as a transport ship. In 1878 and 1879, the ship carried 1,029 tons of exhibits—including streetcars, train cars, and a locomotive—to the Paris Exposition in France. At the Exposition, countries from around the world displayed their newest products.

After the *Constitution* returned to the United States in 1879, Congress began to approve funds to keep the historic ship in good repair. Private groups donated money too. But by 1924, the ship was slowly rotting away in the Charlestown Navy Yard in Boston, Massachusetts. A committee was formed to save the ship. Members began a national campaign to raise money, promote patriotism, and create a stronger bond between U.S. citizens and the historic ship. The campaign came up short, but Congress approved more money. In the end, almost $1 million was raised to restore the ship. To thank contributors, the U.S. Navy sent the famous ship on a national cruise. Between 1931 and 1934, Old Ironsides was towed to seventy-six cities on the Atlantic, Pacific, and Gulf coasts of the United States.

To get her ready for her two-hundredth birthday, Old Ironsides was restored again. From 1992 to 1996, a $12 million restoration strengthened the ship. In July of 1997, a crew of about 150 sailed her for the first time in 116 years. Children and adults across the United States

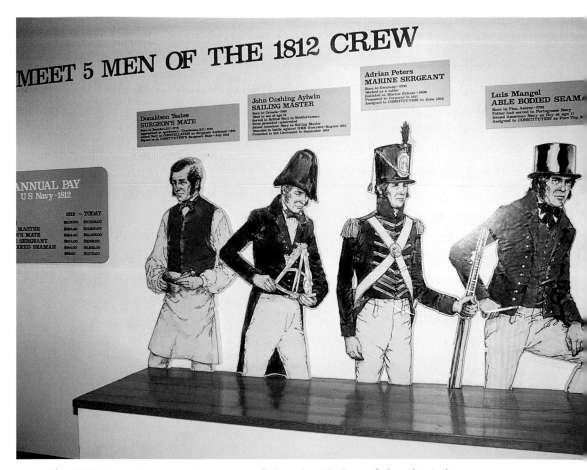

The USS Constitution *Museum exhibits highlights of the ship's history and information about the 1812 crew.*

contributed to a pennies campaign that raised more than $150,000 to buy six new sails.

In modern times, Old Ironsides is docked in the Charlestown Naval Yard. Across the pier, visitors can tour the USS *Constitution* Museum with its interesting exhibits about the historic ship. Thousands of people travel to Boston every year to see the world's oldest commissioned warship still afloat.

Visitors can tour the USS Constitution *Museum and the ship itself to discover how life was on Old Ironsides.*

Glossary

aft: Toward the back of a boat

bilge: The lowest part of a ship's hull

binnacle: The box near the ship's helm where the compass is kept

bulwark: The side of a ship that rises above the top deck

carronade: A short gun (cannon)

course: A ship's planned travel pattern

frigate: A warship with guns on two decks—the spar deck and the gun deck

galley: A ship's kitchen

gangplank: A movable bridge that links a ship to a pier

helm: A ship's steering equipment, especially the wheel that controls the rudder.

HMS: His (or Her) Majesty's Ship

hull: The body of a ship, not including the mast, rigging, and yards

man-of-war: A navy's warship

mast: A tall pole rising from the deck of a sailing ship that is crossed with yards to support sails

rigging: All of a ship's ropes used in supporting the masts and yards and in adjusting the sails

topsail: The sail above the lowest sail on a mast

yard: A horizontal beam that extends from a mast that holds up a sail

Further Reading

Brown, Duncan. *The Monkey's Constitution*. Sandwich, MA: Discovery Enterprises, 1997.

Martin, Tyrone G. *A Most Fortunate Ship: A Narrative History of Old Ironsides*. Annapolis, MD: U.S. Naval Institute Press, 1997.

Robbins, Jerry. *Old Ironsides and the Barbary Pirates*. The Colonial Radio Theatre On the Air, 1996, audiocassette.

Weitzman, David. *Old Ironsides: America Builds a Fighting Ship*. Boston, MA: Houghton Mifflin, 1997.

Touring Information

The USS *Constitution* Museum is open year-round, every day except for Thanksgiving, December 25, and January 1. Between November 1 and April 30, the USS *Constitution* Museum is open from 10 A.M. to 4 P.M., and between May 1 and October 31, the museum is open from 9 A.M. to 6 P.M. The USS *Constitution* is open from 9:30 A.M. until 15 minutes before sundown. For more information,

write to:
USS *Constitution* Museum
P.O. Box 1812
Boston, MA 02129

or call: (617) 426-1812

or visit the website at:
<http://www.ussconstitution.navy.mil/visitorinfo>

Index

About the Author

Robert Young, a prolific author of children's books, created the *How It Was* series to enable readers to tour famous landmarks through the experiences of people who did or may have lived, worked, or visited there. Robert, who makes his home in Eugene, Oregon, teaches elementary school and visits schools around the country to talk with students about writing and curiosity. Among his other literary credits are *Money* and *Game Day*, titles published by Carolrhoda Books, Inc.

Acknowledgments

For quoted material: pp. 5, 23, Tyrone G., *A Most Fortunate Ship*. (Chester, CT: The Globe Pequot Press, 1980); pp. 45, 55, "The Broadside Ballad," reprinted in Gruppe, Henry E., *The Frigates* (Alexandria, VA: Time-Life Books, Inc. 1979); p. 33, Holmes, Oliver Wendell. "Old Ironsides," as quoted in Martin, Tyrone G., *A Most Fortunate Ship*.

For photos and artwork: © Grace Davies Photography, p. 1; © Eliot Cohen, pp. 4, 12, 17, 19, 20, 27, 29, 30, 31, 32, 36, 37, 39, 40, 41, 49, 51 (both), 59, 60; © Tony Stone Images/Hulton Getty, pp. 8, 53; © Library of Congress, p. 9; © A.P.S., p. 10 (left); © Independence National Historical Park, p. 10 (right); © JeffGreenberg@juno.com, p. 21; © Dave G. Houser, pp. 22, 44; © INA Corporation Museum, p. 34; Courtesy, Peabody Essex Museum, Salem, MA, p. 54; Courtesy of The Bostonian Society/Old State House, p. 57. All maps and artwork by Bryan Liedahl. Cover photo: © Eliot Cohen.